Canadian Curriculum
ScienceSmart

Grade 5

ISBN: 978-1-927042-87-8

Printed in China

Contents

ISBN: 978-1-927042-87-8

ISBN: 978-1-927042-87-8

ISBN: 978-1-927042-87-8

Human Body Systems

Brain
Heart
Lungs
Stomach
Kidneys
Bones

I can see the major organs in your body clearly.

In this unit, students will:

- identify the major organs, the organ systems, and the functions of the organ systems.
- describe the functions of the brain.
- do exercises on the circulatory system.

1

A. Name each major organ. Then tell which system the major organ belongs.

Major Organ

| brain | heart | kidneys |
| lungs | stomach | bones |

Organ System

circulatory system	urinary system
digestive system	nervous system
respiratory system	skeletal system

1.

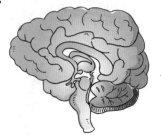

_____

2.

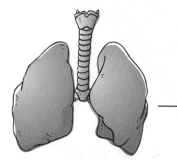

_____

3.

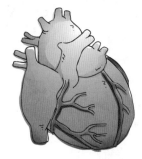

_____

4.

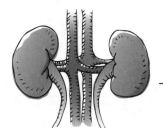

_____

5.

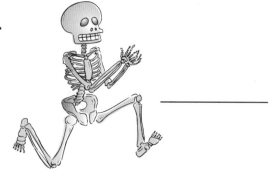

_____

6.

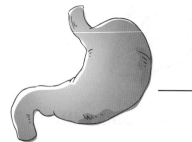

_____

ISBN: 978-1-927042-87-8

B. **Identify the functions of the systems. Name the systems with the help of the given words on the previous page.**

1.

   It is responsible for the ingestion, digestion, and absorption of food.

   _____

2. It delivers nutrients to cells and removes waste.

   _____

3. It controls the body's responses to internal and external stimuli.

   _____

4. It removes waste from the body.

   _____

5. It supports and protects the body.

   _____

6. It is responsible for the exchange of oxygen and carbon dioxide between the body and the environment.

   _____

ISBN: 978-1-927042-87-8

1

C. **Unscramble the letters and write the words on the lines to complete the paragraph. Then fill in the blanks with the given figures.**

Our brain does a number of amazing jobs. It controls

1._____ , 2._____ , 3._____ , and
   aehreatbt   gatrbehin   gtdiesion

many other things that you do

not even think about. It also

allows for 4._____
                thtuogh

and 5._____ to be
        oimoetn

a part of your life.

1.4   41   100 billion   50 000

---

6. The spinal cord, sort of an extension of the brain, is about

   _____ cm long.

7. In our brain, _____ nerve cells link with one another

   using trillions of connections.

8. The adult brain has a mass of _____ kg.

9. In addition to the brain and spinal cord, there are _____ km

   of nerves that carry messages through the body.

D. **Fill in the blanks with the given words to complete the paragraph. Then put a check mark in the circle if the sentence is correct; otherwise, put a cross 5.**

circulatory   diseases   carbon dioxide   oxygen

oxygen

carbon dioxide

All the cells in our bodies need 1._____

to survive and to get rid of waste materials such as

2._____ . The 3._____

system does that as well as fights infections and

4._____ .

5. A capillary is a microscopic thin-walled blood vessel. ◯

6. The heart is the major pumping organ in the body. ◯

7. Blood is carried to the heart in arteries. ◯

8. Veins carry blood away from the heart. ◯

9. Oxygen is a gas needed by our cells in order to carry out their jobs. ◯

10. Carbon dioxide is a waste gas produced by cells as they break down food. ◯

ISBN: 978-1-927042-87-8

1

My Heart Rate

Our heart helps circulate blood to and from all parts of our body. The blood carries nutrients and oxygen to all cells in a network of arteries and veins. When we exercise, our cells need more oxygen and nutrients, so our heart pumps faster. Follow the steps below to measure your heart rate.

Steps to check your heart rate:

1. Check your resting heart rate by locating your pulse in your wrist.

   15 seconds

2. Count the number of beats in 15 seconds.

3. Multiply the number by 4 to get your heart rate in beats per minute (bpm).

4. Run up and down stairs for 1 minute. Check your heart rate (bpm) again.

Resting Heart Rate (bpm): _____   **Heart Rate after Exercise (bpm):** _____

Are you able to...

- [ ] identify the major organs, the organ systems, and the functions of the organ systems?
- [ ] describe the functions of the brain?
- [ ] complete the exercises on the circulatory system?

ISBN: 978-1-927042-87-8

Respiratory System and Skeletal System

In this unit, students will:

- study and label the diagram of the respiratory system.
- identify the parts in the respiratory system.
- study and label the diagram of the skeletal system.
- tell some facts related to bones.

ISBN: 978-1-927042-87-8

2

A. Fill in the blanks with the given words. Then label the diagram.

The respiratory system helps deliver _____ to all the cells in our body. It also removes _____ , a waste product, from our body.

Science Corner . . . .

The maximum volume of air that our lungs can hold is called our "lung capacity".

bronchioles   bronchial tubes
alveoli   lungs   trachea
nose   diaphragm

Respiratory System

1. _____

2. _____

3. _____

4. _____

5. _____

6. _____

7. _____

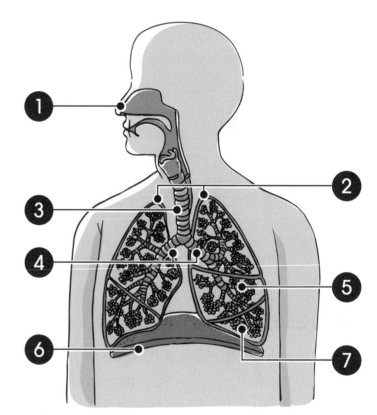

ISBN: 978-1-927042-87-8

B. Match the descriptions with the parts in the respiratory system. Write the names on the lines with the help of the given words on the previous page.

1. a place where air is moistened and cleaned as it enters the body

   _____

2. the two branches of the trachea

   _____

3. a thin dome-shaped muscle which draws downward on inhalation and pushes upward in exhalation

   _____

4. breathing organs that bring oxygen to and remove carbon dioxide from the blood

   _____

5. the tube to the bronchial tubes and lungs

   _____

6. small tubes of the bronchial tubes

   _____

7.

   They're small air sacs that allow oxygen to enter and carbon dioxide to leave the body.

   _____

2

C. Fill in the blanks with the given words. Then label the diagram.

| organs | support | muscles |

The skeletal system gives our body

1._____ and protects our

2._____ . Working closely

with 3._____ , it allows us to move.

Skeletal System

4.

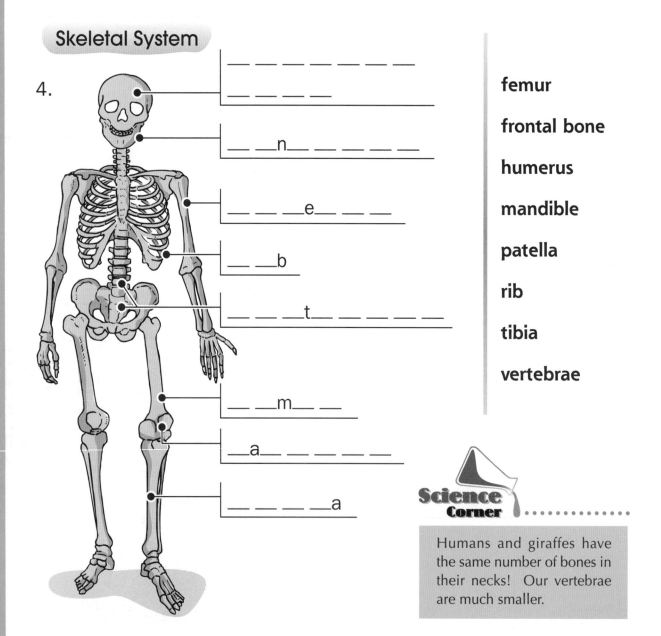

_ _ _ _ _ _ _ _
_ _ _ _ _

_ _ _n_ _ _ _ _ _

_ _ _ _e_ _ _ _

_ _ _b

_ _ _ _t_ _ _ _ _ _

_ _ _m_ _ _

_ _a_ _ _ _ _ _

_ _ _ _ _a

femur

frontal bone

humerus

mandible

patella

rib

tibia

vertebrae

Science Corner . . . .

Humans and giraffes have the same number of bones in their necks! Our vertebrae are much smaller.

   ISBN: 978-1-927042-87-8

D. Circle the correct words to complete the sentences.

1. _____ and bones work together to allow for movement.

   Blood / Muscles / Hair

2. The long bones in our body are _____ , which makes them light and strong.

   solid / hand / hollow

3. Before our bones turned into bones, they were _____ .

   cartilage / blood / tissue

4. More than _____ bones make up the hollow shape that is our skull.

   5 / 20 / 250

5. _____ , which makes blood cells, is found in all the bones of babies and some adult bones.

   Calcium / Tissue / Marrow

6. The largest bone is femur, which is our _____ .

   thigh bone / frontal bone / humerus

2

Finding Your Lung Capacity

Here is a way to find your lung capacity.

Materials:

- a big tank
- a plastic jar with a lid
- water
- a plastic tube

Steps:

1. Fill the big tank halfway with water.

2. Completely fill the plastic jar with water. Tighten the lid. Turn over the jar and put it in the tank of water. Remove the lid.

3. Take a plastic tube and feed one end of it up into the inverted jar.

4. Take a deep breath and blow hard through the other end of the tube. You can see that the water in the jar is displaced by air.

5. Tighten the lid again and remove the jar from the tank of water. Use a measuring cup to fill the jar with water again. The volume of water you need to fill it back up is your lung capacity.

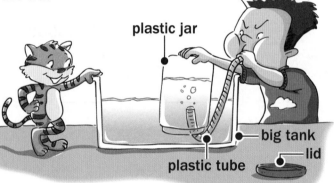

plastic jar

big tank

lid

plastic tube

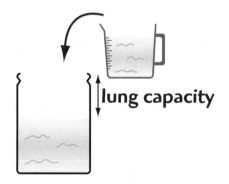

lung capacity

Are you able to...

- [ ] explain and label the diagram of the respiratory system?
- [ ] identify the parts in the respiratory system?
- [ ] explain and label the diagram of the skeletal system?
- [ ] tell some facts related to bones?

ISBN: 978-1-927042-87-8

Digestive System and Excretory System

In this unit, students will:

- study and label the diagram of the digestive system.
- identify the process of digestion.
- study and label the diagram of the urinary system.
- identify the organs in the excretory system.

ISBN: 978-1-927042-87-8

3

A. Fill in the blanks with the given words. Then label the diagram.

energy   food   cells

We get energy from 1._____ .
The digestive system breaks down
food into very tiny parts so that all the
2._____ in our body can get the
3._____ they need.

4.

Digestive System

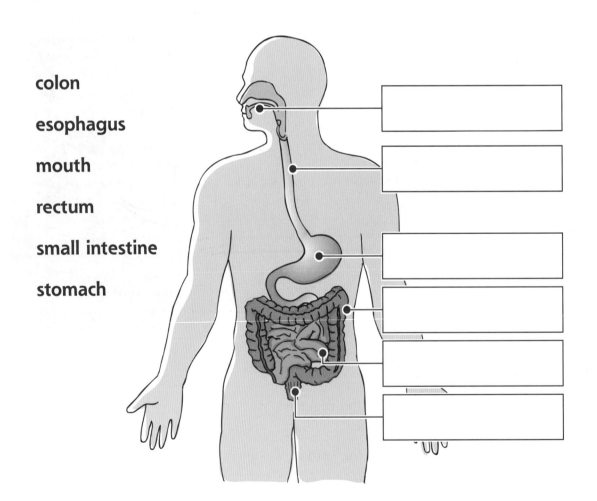

colon

esophagus

mouth

rectum

small intestine

stomach

ISBN: 978-1-927042-87-8

B. **Write 1 to 6 to show the journey of a pear as it is eaten and digested.**

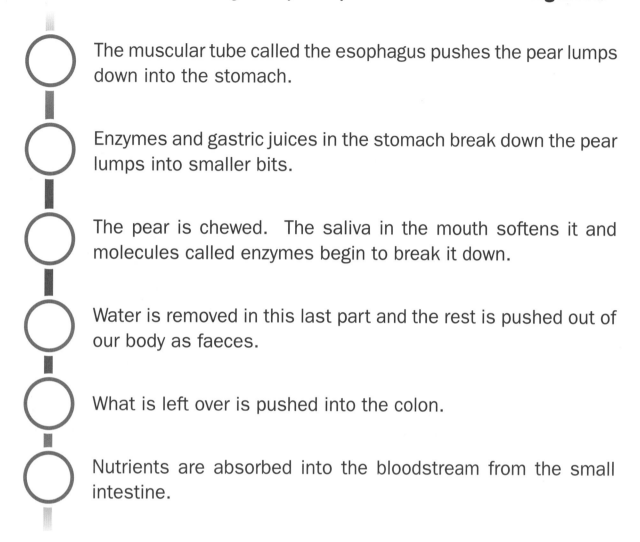

○ The muscular tube called the esophagus pushes the pear lumps down into the stomach.

○ Enzymes and gastric juices in the stomach break down the pear lumps into smaller bits.

○ The pear is chewed. The saliva in the mouth softens it and molecules called enzymes begin to break it down.

○ Water is removed in this last part and the rest is pushed out of our body as faeces.

○ What is left over is pushed into the colon.

○ Nutrients are absorbed into the bloodstream from the small intestine.

C. **See which digestive organs the children are talking about. Write the names of the organs on the lines.**

1.

The body absorbs most nutrients when the food is there.

_____

2.

After the body takes the nutrients, the food goes through this to have any extra water removed.

_____

3

D. **Read the paragraph. Then label the diagram with the words in bold.**

*The urinary system pushes water and other waste products out of our body. It consists of two **kidneys**: one on each side of our body. They filter the blood and remove waste materials and excess water from our body in the form of urine. The urine travels down the **ureters** and empty into a bag-like organ called **bladder**. Urine is temporarily stored in this stretched organ. From there, the collected urine passes out of the body through the **urethra**.*

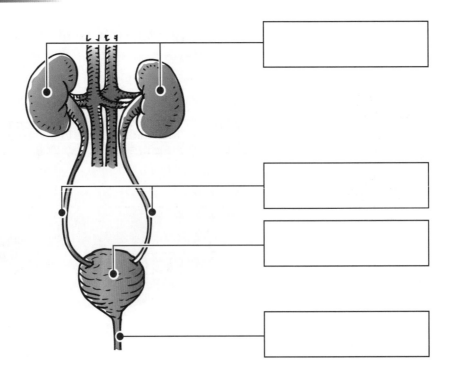

Urinary System

ISBN: 978-1-927042-87-8

E. Read the paragraph on the previous page again. Tell the functions or roles of the following organs.

1. kidneys _____

2. bladder _____

3. ureters _____

4. urethra _____

F. Read what Jossie says. Then write the answers.

The excretory system is the group of organs that get rid of waste products in our body. Kidneys are the most important organs in this system. Our skin and lungs also help.

When we sweat, our skin gets rid of excess water and salt. That way, it keeps our body cool. When we breathe, we take in oxygen and breathe out carbon dioxide, a waste product. Our kidneys filter out some waste products and extra salt from our blood and make urine, which helps keep a balance of salt and water in our body.

1. The organs in our excretory system:

_____

2. The organs that get rid of carbon dioxide: _____

3. The organs that filter cell wastes from the blood: _____

4. The organ that keeps our body cool by getting rid of excess water and salt: _____

3

The Digestive System Fun Facts

Play this game with your friends to see who knows more about our digestive system.

1. About how many litres of saliva are produced a day?

   A. 1.7 litres   **B.** 8 litres   **C.** 0.2 litre

2. About how many litres of material can the stomach of an adult hold?

   A. 0.5 litre   **B.** 1.5 litres   **C.** 5 litres

3. About how long is the esophagus of an adult?

   A. 68 cm   **B.** 4 cm   **C.** 25 cm

4. How long does it take for the human body to digest a high fat meal?

   A. 6 hours   **B.** 15 minutes   **C.** 2 days

5. How long may the food stay in the small intestine?

   A. 4 hours   **B.** 5 minutes   **C.** 1 day

6. About how long is the small intestine?

   A. 6.5 m   **B.** 6.5 cm   **C.** 16 m

If you can answer these questions correctly, you are really a "digestive system" expert!

Answers: 1. A   2. B   3. C   4. A   5. A   6. A

Are you able to...

- [ ] explain and label the diagram of the digestive system?
- [ ] identify the process of digestion?
- [ ] explain and label the diagram of the urinary system?
- [ ] identify the organs in the excretory system?

ISBN: 978-1-927042-87-8

Nutrition

In this unit, students will:

- identify different kinds of nutrients in foods and their functions in maintaining a healthy body.
- identify a balanced diet as one containing carbohydrates, proteins, fats, minerals, vitamins, fibres, and water, and design a diet that contains all of them.

ISBN: 978-1-927042-87-8

4

A. Read each of the following and unscramble the name of the nutrient. Then draw a food item that is a source of that nutrient.

When we eat, we get the things that our body systems need to function properly. We need nutrients to live. For example, fibre is a nutrient found in plants. It plays an important role in our digestive processes.

1. These nutrients keep our cells healthy. Some of them can be stored by the body, but some can't. They are found in fruits and vegetables.

——————————————
itviamns

2. This is needed for cells to work properly. It is also used to carry nutrients through the body. It can be found in juicy fruits.

——————————————
atwer

3.

These nutrients are found in most foods and are needed for nerve cells and other types of cells to remain healthy. The body can save them to store energy. They can be found in things like salad dressings and margarine.

——————————————
afts

ISBN: 978-1-927042-87-8

4. These are good for teeth and bone growth. They are found in fruits, vegetables, and milk.

_____
snmiaerl

5. They include starches and sugars that are broken down to form glucose, the main form of energy used by the cells of the body. They can be found in bread and rice.

_____
etcboydrahras

6.

We need them because they are used by cells for repair and growth. Meat, fish, cheese, nuts, and beans are sources of these nutrients.

_____
spenorti

B. Look at each food item. Then name two nutrients that can be found in it.

1.

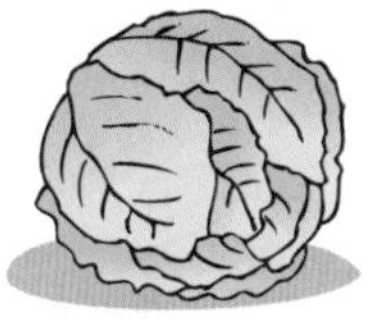

2.

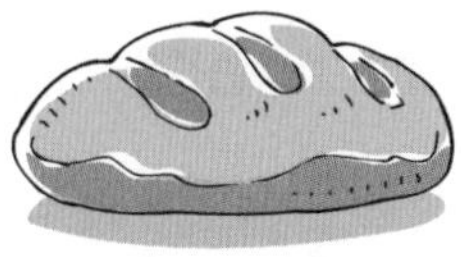

3.

_____   _____   _____

_____   _____   _____

4

C. **Look at the chart and see what each child eats on a typical day. Then answer the questions.**

Recommended Number of Food Guide Servings Per Day
(Children: between 9 and 13 years old)

Vegetables and Fruits
6 – 7 servings

Grain Products
6 – 7 servings

Milk and Alternatives
3 – 4 servings

Meat and Alternatives
1 – 2 servings

Sam

Breakfast: sugar coated cereal, chocolate milk, and candy apple

Lunch: pizza, potato chips, and chocolate doughnut

Dinner: barbecued pork sausage and potatoes with butter

Lucy

Breakfast: oatmeal cereal, banana, and milk

Lunch: bagel, cream cheese, yogourt, apple, and water

Dinner: fish, rice, pasta, carrots, broccoli, and vegetable soup

1. Who is eating the right foods?

   _____

It is important to eat the right foods for proper growth and good health.

2. What changes would you suggest to make the other child's diet more healthful?

   _____

   _____

   _____

D. **Read what Chris says. Use the information provided on the previous page to help Chris plan his meals for a week. Then check the healthful snack foods.**

I'm a Grade 5 student. I always eat breakfast and dinner at home, and take my lunch to school every day. Please help me choose the right foods to eat from a variety of foods. Don't forget to include fibre-rich food such as cereal and apples in my diet.

Chris

	Breakfast	**Lunch**	**Dinner**
Monday			
Tuesday			
Wednesday			
Thursday			
Friday			

Healthful Snack Foods:

A chocolate chip cookies   B graham crackers

C fat-free pudding   D ice cream bar

E potato chips   F rice cakes

Nutrition Facts

Take a look around your house and find packaged food for the nutrition facts table. Enter the data of any two food items in the tables provided below. Compare and describe the nutrients in these two food items.

Food:

Nutrition Facts
per (g)

Amount	% Daily Value
Calories	
Fat g	%
Saturated g	
+Trans g	
Cholesterol mg	
Sodium mg	%
Carbohydrate g	%
Fibre g	
Sugars g	
Protein g	
Vitamin A % Vitamin C	%
Calcium % Iron	%

Food:

Nutrition Facts
per (g)

Amount	% Daily Value
Calories	
Fat g	%
Saturated g	
+Trans g	
Cholesterol mg	
Sodium mg	%
Carbohydrate g	%
Fibre g	
Sugars g	
Protein g	
Vitamin A % Vitamin C	%
Calcium % Iron	%

_____

_____

_____

Are you able to...

☐ identify different kinds of nutrients in foods and their functions in maintaining a healthy body?

☐ identify a balanced diet that contains carbohydrates, proteins, fats, minerals, vitamins, fibres, and water, and design a diet that contains all of them?

Properties of Matter

Thank you, Mr. Ice. You really are cold enough to keep the ice cream frozen even under the sun.

In this unit, students will:

- identify and describe the characteristic properties of each of the three states of matter.
- describe how each state of matter changes to another state.
- describe how the change in temperature changes the state of matter.

ISBN: 978-1-927042-87-8

5

A. **Read what Sue says. Write the missing letters to tell the states and fill in the blanks with the given words to complete the descriptions. Then give an example for each state of matter.**

> Let's look at the way matter behaves. Liquid and gas take the shape of the container they're in, and gas will expand to completely fill a space. Each state of matter has a property or characteristic that makes it different from the other states.

no definite	volume	shape	definite

State   ### Description

1. l__ __ __ __ __

It has a _____ volume but no definite shape.

Example: _____

2. g__ __

It has no definite volume and _____ shape.

Example: _____

3. s__ __ __ __

It has a definite _____ and a definite _____ .

Example: _____

ISBN: 978-1-927042-87-8

B. **Choose the word that describes how each state of matter changes to another state.**

evaporate   freeze   melt

1.

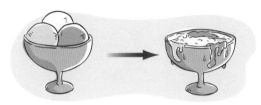

_____

2.

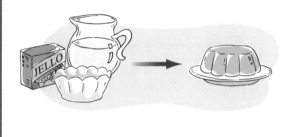

_____

3.

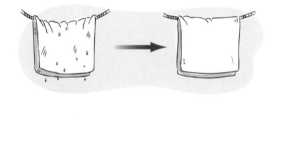

_____

4.

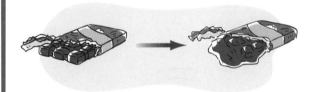

_____

5.

_____

Science Corner

In some cases, a solid may change directly to the gas state, and vice versa. That is called sublimation. An example of this is a household product called Napthalene crystals used to kill moths in stored clothes. The crystals change to vapour directly, which is toxic to moths.

5

C. **What causes the change in state to take place? Tell the states of the matter before and after the changes. Then write "heat taken away" or "heat given" on the lines.**

1.

    _____   _____

    _____   _____

2.

    _____   _____

    _____   _____

3.

    _____   _____

    _____   _____

4.

    _____   _____

    _____   _____

ISBN: 978-1-927042-87-8

D. Fill in the blanks with the given words. Then use the letters in the green boxes to complete what Mary says.

evaporates	melts	condenses	freezes

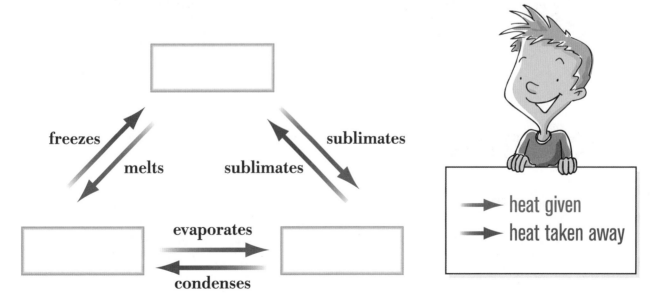

1. Gas __ __ __ __ __ __ __ __ __ to form liquid.

2. Liquid __ __ __ __ __ __ __ __ __ __ to form gas.

3. Solid __ __ __ __ __ to form liquid.

4. Liquid __ __ __ __ __ __ __ to form solid.

5.

For all the changes in the states of matter on the previous page,

it is due to __ha__g__s in __ __ __p__ __atur__ __ .

E. Write "gas", "liquid", or "solid" in the boxes to complete the diagram.

freezes   sublimates

melts   sublimates

evaporates

condenses

→ heat given
→ heat taken away

ISBN: 978-1-927042-87-8

5

Making Solid Cream

You can follow the steps to change the whipping cream to a solid.

Materials:

- heavy whipping cream
- a jar with a tight lid

Steps:

1. Pour about $\frac{1}{4}$ cup of cream into the jar.
2. Tighten the lid and start shaking!
3. Share the shaking with someone!

SHAKE...
SHAKE...
SHAKE...

Checklist

Are you able to...

- [ ] identify and describe the characteristic properties of each of the three states of matter?
- [ ] describe how each state of matter changes to another state?
- [ ] describe how the change in temperature changes the state of matter?

A. Complete the crossword puzzle.

an important organ in our digestive system

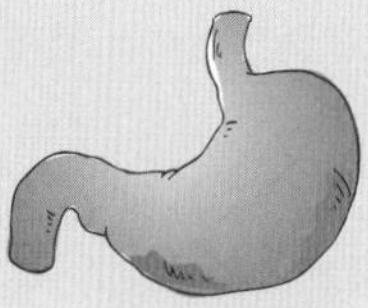

This thin dome-shaped muscle plays an important role in respiration.

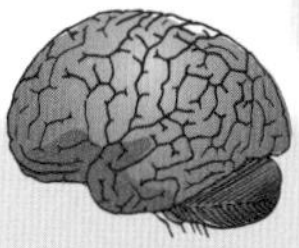

one of our major organs

This muscular tube pushes the chewed food down into the stomach.

These foods are the sources of these nutrients.

the longest bone in our body

Before our bones turned into bones, they were _____ .

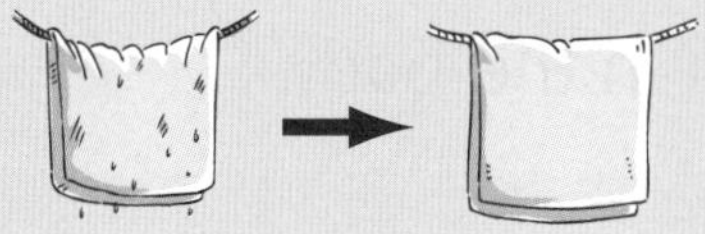

evaporates   brain   carbohydrates   cartilage

diaphragm   esophagus   femur   stomach

ISBN: 978-1-927042-87-8

B. Check the correct answers.

1. Foods that are sources of protein:

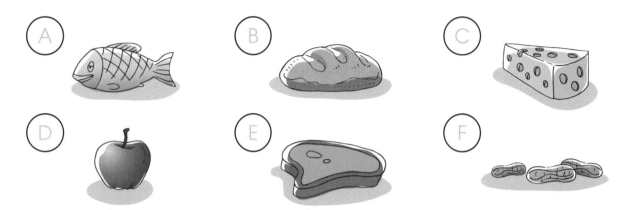

2. The ones that show melting:

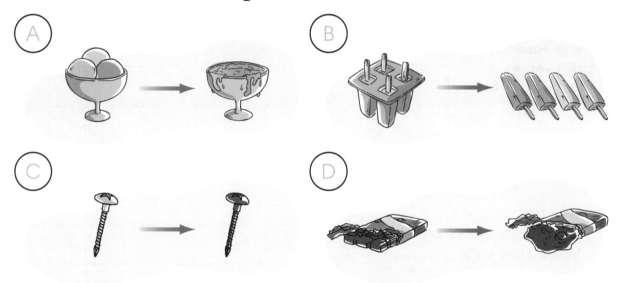

3. The correct sentences that describe our circulatory system:

   A   The heart is the major pumping organ in the body.

   B   Veins carry blood away from the body.

   C   Oxygen is a gas needed by our cells to function properly.

   D   Our circulatory system is a system that fights diseases and infections.

ISBN: 978-1-927042-87-8

4. The names of the organs in our digestive system:

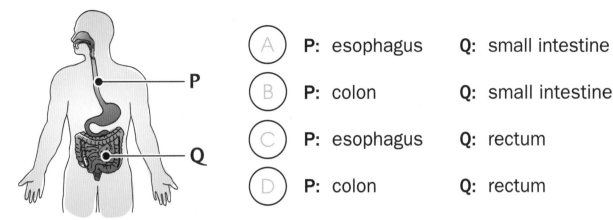

- (A) **P:** esophagus   **Q:** small intestine
- (B) **P:** colon   **Q:** small intestine
- (C) **P:** esophagus   **Q:** rectum
- (D) **P:** colon   **Q:** rectum

5. The major organs in our respiratory system:

- (A) diaphragm
- (B) lungs
- (C) esophagus
- (D) heart
- (E) kidneys
- (F) trachea

6. The names of the organs in our urinary system:

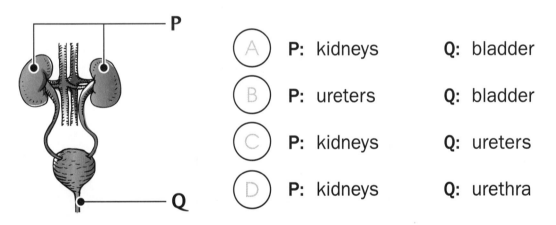

- (A) **P:** kidneys   **Q:** bladder
- (B) **P:** ureters   **Q:** bladder
- (C) **P:** kidneys   **Q:** ureters
- (D) **P:** kidneys   **Q:** urethra

7. The states of water shown below:

- (A) **1** liquid   **2** solid
- (B) **1** solid   **2** gas
- (C) **1** solid   **2** liquid
- (D) **1** gas   **2** liquid

ISBN: 978-1-927042-87-8

C. Write the given words under the appropriate systems.

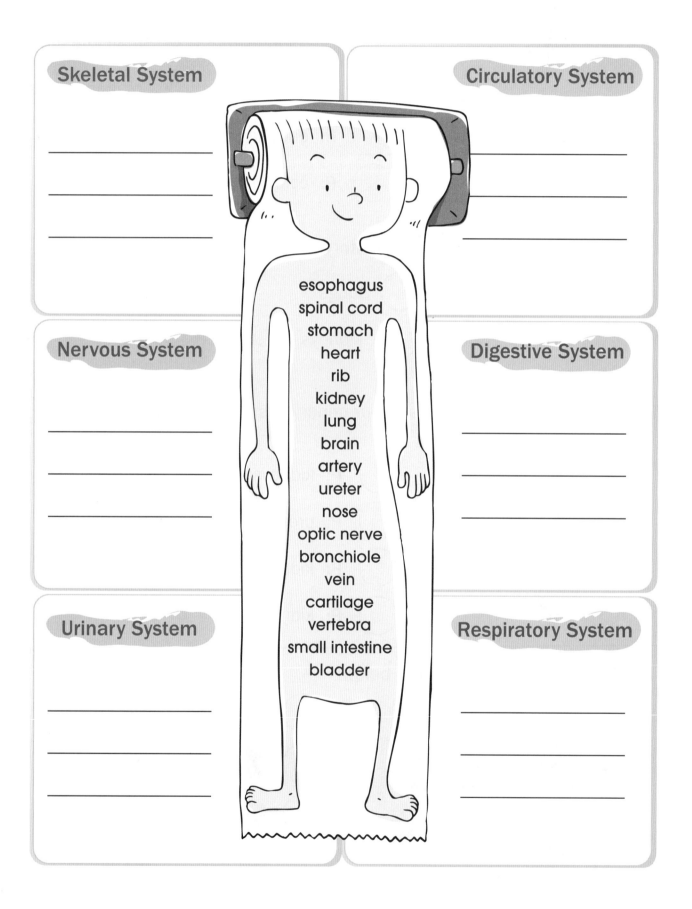

Skeletal System

Circulatory System

Nervous System

Digestive System

Urinary System

Respiratory System

esophagus
spinal cord
stomach
heart
rib
kidney
lung
brain
artery
ureter
nose
optic nerve
bronchiole
vein
cartilage
vertebra
small intestine
bladder

ISBN: 978-1-927042-87-8

Changes in Matter

In this unit, students will:

- identify "physical change" and "chemical change" in matter.
- identify changes as reversible or irreversible.
- choose the appropriate instruments to measure matter in different forms.
- put things in order of density.
- solve problems about mass and states of matter.

6

A. **Fill in the blanks with the given words. Then write "physical change" or "chemical change" for each change of matter.**

chemical	state	physical	colour

When something changes, it can be a physical change or a chemical

change. While a 1._____ change is a change in substance, a

2._____ change means a change in shape, 3._____ ,

size, etc. The substance remains the same. When the 4._____

of matter changes, that is a physical change. Water, ice, and water vapour

are still all water.

5.

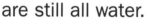

_____

physical change

6.

_____

7.

_____

8.

_____

ISBN: 978-1-927042-87-8

B. **Look at the pictures. Write whether these changes are "reversible" or "irreversible".**

An ice cube that melts can be changed to a solid again, just as evaporated water may once again be liquid. These changes are reversible. Some changes, like chemical changes, are irreversible.

reversible

1.

_____

2.

_____

3.

_____

4.

_____

5.

_____

ISBN: 978-1-927042-87-8

6

C. What would you use to measure each of the following forms of matter? Match the matter with the correct instrument. Write the letter.

To find...

1. the dimensions of a bed ◯

2. the volume of a water bottle ◯

3. the mass of a cup ◯

4. the height of a box ◯

5. the mass of a block ◯

6. the volume of a sink ◯

Science Corner

Weight is different from mass. An object's weight has to do with its mass and the pull gravity on it. You have a different weight on the moon from your weight on Earth, but your mass is exactly the same no matter where you are.

D. Put the things in order of density. Start with the one that has the least density.

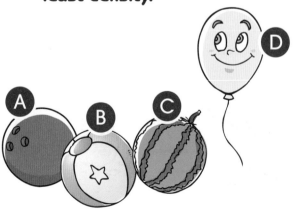

An object can have a great amount of mass, and yet be very small. The amount of mass something has, in a particular volume or space, is called density.

In order: _____

ISBN: 978-1-927042-87-8

E. Read what Salina says. Then circle the correct answer to each of these mass mysteries.

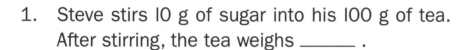

A change in state does not mean a change in mass. Matter cannot disapper or appear. Similarly, when mixtures are formed, the mass of one is added to the other.

1. Steve stirs 10 g of sugar into his 100 g of tea. After stirring, the tea weighs _____ .

   110 g   more than 110 g   less than 100 g

2. Mrs. Cook covered a bowl of soup with a plastic wrap. Later some of the water in the soup evaporated and condensed on the inside of the wrap. The mass of the bowl, soup, and the plastic wrap together has _____ .

   increased   decreased   stayed the same

3. A glass of orange juice with 3 ice cubes in it weighs 250 g. After the ice cubes melt, it weighs _____ .

   250 g   less than 250 g   more than 250 g

4. Marcus makes a frozen treat by putting some juice in the freezer. When he takes it out, he finds that the volume of the frozen juice is a bit greater than when it was liquid. With freezing, the mass of the juice _____ .

   decreased   increased   stayed the same

ISBN: 978-1-927042-87-8

6

Layers of Liquids

> In this experiment, you can find out which liquid, water, oil, or honey, has the greatest density.

Materials:

- a cup of water, a cup of oil, and a cup of honey
- a big glass jar

Steps:

1. Pour the honey into the jar.

2. Pour the water into the jar.

3. Pour the oil into the jar.

4. Wait for all three substances to settle.

> The one with the greatest density goes to the bottom and the one with the least density goes to the top.

Put the liquids in order from the one that has the greatest density to the one that has the least.

_____

Checklist

Are you able to...

- [ ] identify "physical change" and "chemical change" in matter?
- [ ] identify changes as reversible or irreversible?
- [ ] choose the appropriate instruments to measure matter in different forms?
- [ ] put things in order of density?
- [ ] solve problems about mass and states of matter?

Forces and Structures (1)

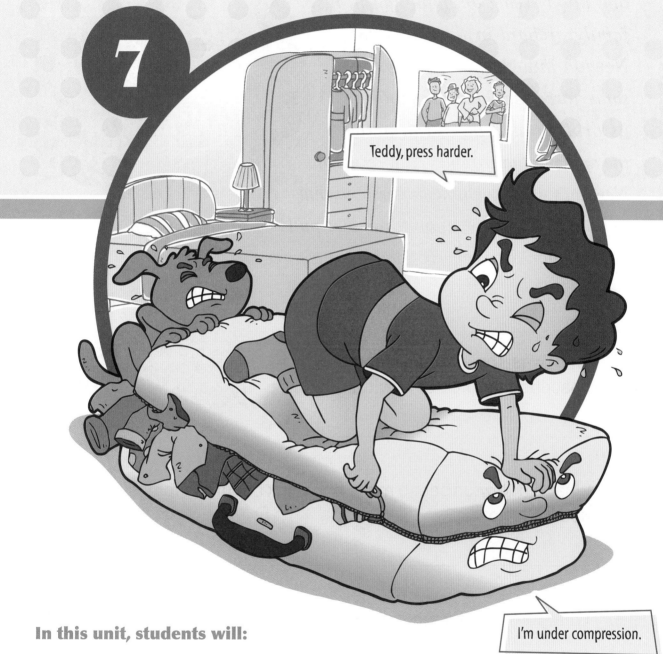

In this unit, students will:

- answer questions about the force of gravity.
- draw arrows to show the directions of the forces pulled by gravity.
- complete sentences about structures and forces.
- learn the meanings of tension and compression.
- label each part of a structure that is under either compression or tension.

ISBN: 978-1-927042-87-8

7

A. Read the paragraph. Then answer the questions.

Sir Isaac Newton was the first person to describe the force of gravity. A story tells that upon seeing an apple fall in his family orchard in the mid-1660s, Newton thought that perhaps the same force that held the moon in its orbit around the Earth pulled the apple to the ground. As a result of Newton's work, we now understand that the force of gravity is the force that pulls objects upon other objects. Matter exerts force on each other.

One of the forces that are upon everything is the force of gravity.

1. Who was the first person to describe the force of gravity?

   _____

2. What did Newton see to make him think about the forces that pulled upon each other?

   _____

3. What force pulled the apple to the ground?

   _____

4. What is the force of gravity?

   _____

ISBN: 978-1-927042-87-8

B. **This is the Earth. Look at the people on it. Are any of them about to fall off? Draw arrows from the people to show the direction in which they are being pulled by gravity.**

C. **Complete the sentences with the help of the given words.**

spoke	torque	Newton	inclined plane

1. Metre is to length as _____ is to force.

2. Lever is to see-saw as _____ is to playground slide.

3. _____ is to jar lid as pull is to cork.

4. Beam is to bridge as _____ is to bicycle wheel.

ISBN: 978-1-927042-87-8

7

D. **Fill in the blanks with the given words. Then identify the pictures that show either compression or tension. Write "compression" or "tension" on the lines.**

compression	tension	pushing	pulling	force of gravity

All structures on Earth must deal with the 1._____ . They must also be able to withstand additional forces that come into play when the structures are in use. Structures are always either in 2._____ or 3._____ . Compression is a 4._____ force. Tension is a 5._____ force.

6.

_____

7.

_____

8.

_____

9.

_____

ISBN: 978-1-927042-87-8

E. Label each part of the structures that is under "compression" or "tension".

1. **Computer Desk**

a.

b.

c.

d.

2. **Bridge**

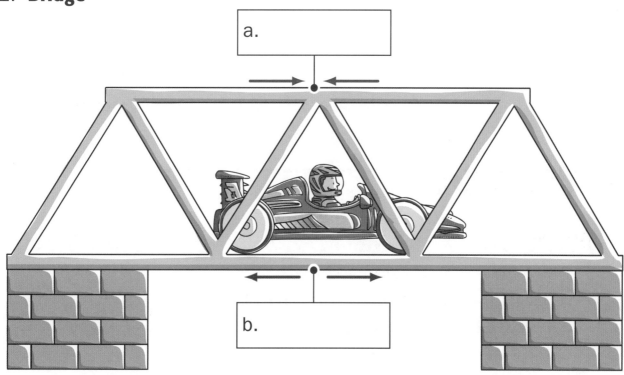

a.

b.

7

My Special Nest

Design and construct a structure that will protect your egg from a fall.

> Build a structure with the listed materials to protect an egg. When completed, it should be able to survive a drop of up to 2 metres off the floor.

> Let me ask my mom to give us some eggs to test our nest.

Here's a place to sketch out your plan. Design it. Build it. Test it.

Materials:

- tape
- glue
- straws
- elastic bands
- paper clips
- cardboard

Are you able to...

☐ answer questions about the force of gravity?

☐ draw arrows to show the directions of the forces pulled by gravity?

☐ complete sentences about structures and forces?

☐ explain what tension and compression are?

☐ label each part of a structure that is under either compression or tension?

Forces and Structures (2)

8

I want to cut these flowers for my mom. If I use a pair of scissors with longer arms, I can gain mechanical advantage because when the distance between the effort and the fulcrum increases, the output force is increased as well.

fulcrum

longer distance

fulcrum

shorter distance

In this unit, students will:

- choose the machines that have mechanical advantages to do the assigned jobs.
- identify the components of a recording system and understand that changing one component in a system will make the system change.

8

A. Read what the workmen say. Help them choose the most suitable machine in each group. Put a check mark in the circle. Then answer the question.

> Structures sometimes have mechanical systems attached to them. Mechanical systems are systems that make use of one or more simple machines. Mechanical advantage is a measurement that we use to describe how much easier it is to move or lift a load with the use of a mechanical system.

1.

> I'm going to lift the load.

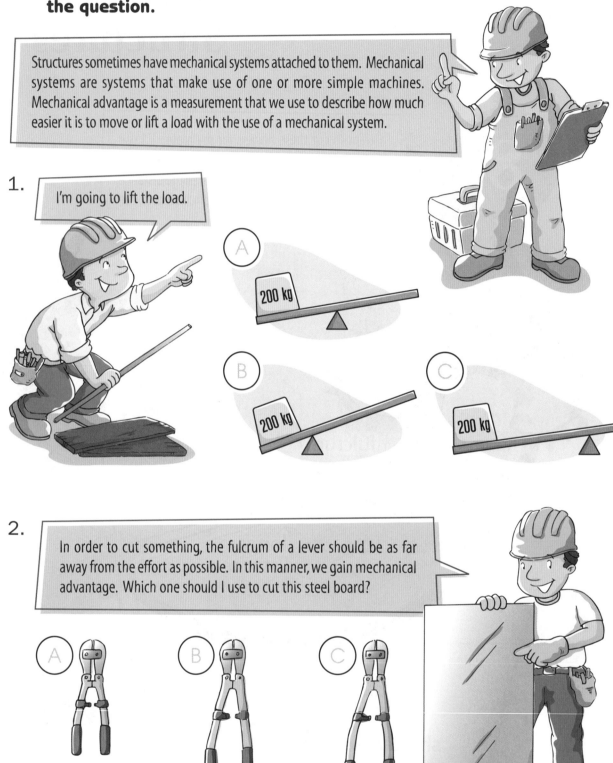

2.

> In order to cut something, the fulcrum of a lever should be as far away from the effort as possible. In this manner, we gain mechanical advantage. Which one should I use to cut this steel board?

3. Why do they choose these machines?

_____

ISBN: 978-1-927042-87-8

B. **Read what each workman says. Put a check mark in the circle if it is correct; otherwise, put a cross and rewrite the statement.**

1.

Changing a part of the system will change how well the system as a whole does the job that it is supposed to do.

_____

_____

_____

2.

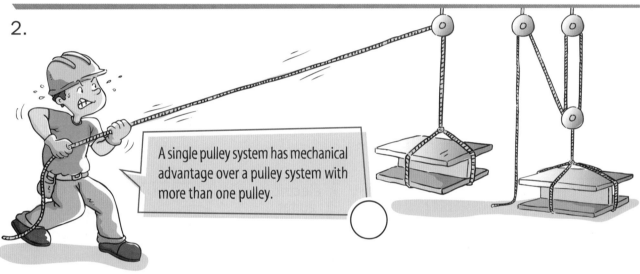

A single pulley system has mechanical advantage over a pulley system with more than one pulley.

_____

3.

Mechanical advantage cannot be gained by using gears of different sizes.

_____

_____

_____

8

C. **Read what Glen says. Look at his recording system and the descriptions. Trace the dotted lines that represent wires. Then answer the questions.**

I run a recording studio. Musicians come in and I record and produce their music using my computer. My system is made up of many parts, or components. These components must work together to ensure that the jobs they are designed to do will be done.

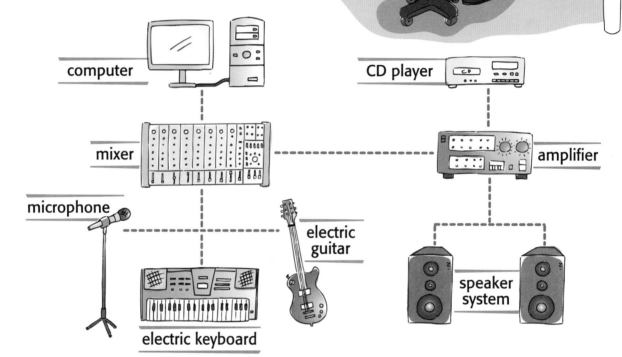

computer

CD player

mixer

amplifier

microphone

electric guitar

electric keyboard

speaker system

Components

1. __ __m__ __t__ __ :

   This component mixes and records music.

2. m__ __e__ :

   Electrical signals arrive here to be sent to other places.

3. __m__ __if__e__ :

   The strength of signals passing through it is increased here.

4. __p__ __ke__ s__ __te__ :
   This system turns electrical signals coming from the amplifier into sound energy.

5. __D p__ __y__ __ :
   It plays the finished product.

6. __i__ __op__ __n__ :
   It takes sound waves and turns them into electrical signals.

7. el__ __tr__ __ g__i__ __ __ and __ __ybo__ __d:
   They are electronic instruments.

8. How many components are there in a recording system?

   _____

9. Describe the forces that the microphone must be able to withstand.

   _____

10. I played a song and recorded it on the computer, but no sound is coming out of the speakers. Suggest two reasons for this problem.

    _____

    _____

    _____

11. If one of these components starts to malfunction or break, what will be its effect on the rest of the system?

    _____

8

An Amazing Inclined Plane

Materials:

- 3 telephone directories

- 3 wooden boards of different lengths

- a can of food in the shape of a rectangular prism

- a string

Do you know how to gain the mechanical advantage of an inclined plane?

Steps:

1. Put the directories in a pile.

2. Lay the shortest board against the piled-up directories.

3. Tie the can with the string.

4. Pull the can up the board slowly.

5. Then do the same with the other two boards.

On which board did you need the least effort to pull up the can? Do you know why?

_____

_____

Checklist

Are you able to...

☐ choose the machines that have mechanical advantages to do the assigned jobs?

☐ identify the components of a recording system and understand that changing one component in a system will make the system change?

    ISBN: 978-1-927042-87-8

Conservation of Energy (1)

In this unit, students will:

- identify energy suppliers.
- define, identify, and give examples of different forms of energy.
- identify kinetic energy and potential energy.
- find the energy input and energy output for different energy converters.

9

A. Name the energy supplier in each picture.

— Energy Supplier —

batteries	food	gasoline
the sun	wind	wood

Scientists say that the universe is made up of two things, matter and energy. Matter is the "stuff" from which all things are made. The ability to make this "stuff" move and do work is called "energy".

1.

_____

2.

_____

3.

_____

4.

_____

5.

_____

6.

_____

ISBN: 978-1-927042-87-8

B. Match the definitions with the different forms of energy. Write the names of energy on the lines.

Form of Energy

chemical	heat	wind	light
electrical	sound	gravitational	

1.

> the energy that is produced by chemical reaction

_____

2. the energy that an object has because it is above the Earth's surface

_____

3. the energy that is found in moving air   _____

4. the energy that is produced by the vibration of an object   _____

5. the energy that hot objects have more than cold objects   _____

6. the energy used by washing machines, dryers, and televisions   _____

7. the energy that allows us to see things   _____

9

C. **Identify three forms of energy that you use in your house. Give an example for each.**

Form of Energy	Example
_____	_____
_____	_____
_____	_____

D. **Unscramble the letters to write the energy words. Then tell whether each picture shows "kinetic energy" or "potential energy".**

1. When something is moving, it has an energy that is known as

    _____ energy. A moving object can do work.
    ciekint

2. _____ energy of an object is the stored energy of the
    aittPoenl
    object. It is hard to see.

3.

    _____

4.

    _____

5.

    _____

6.

    _____

ISBN: 978-1-927042-87-8

E. Find the correct energy input and energy output for each energy converter.

——— **Energy Input** ———

electrical   chemical
gravitational

——— **Energy Output** ———

sound   light and heat
heat   electrical

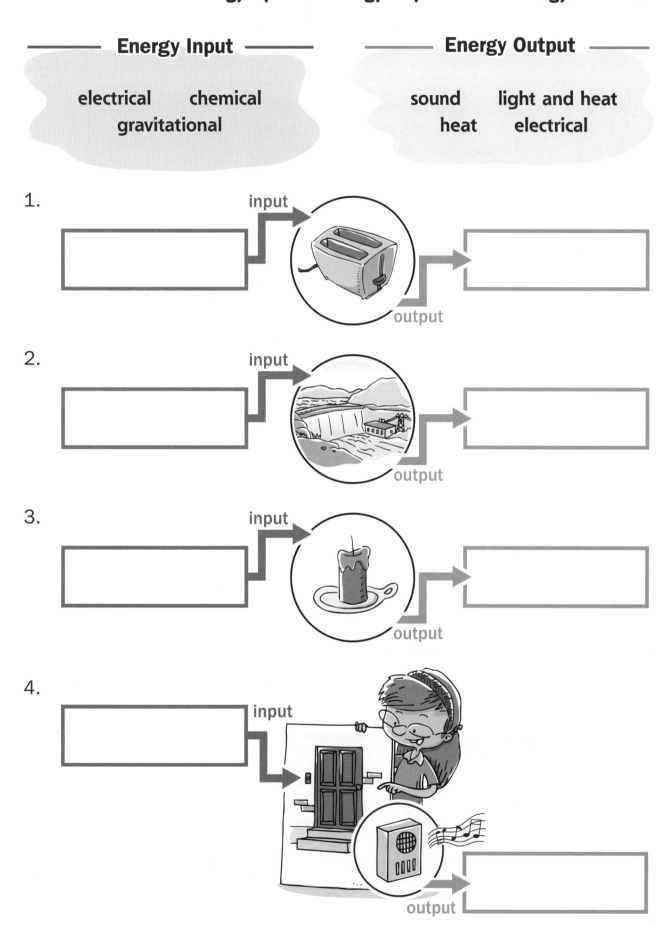

1. input | output

2. input | output

3. input | output

4. input | output

9

Pop the Cork!

> In this experiment, you can see how the cork pops out of the bottle. Do you know what forms of energy are involved in this experiment?

Materials:

- bathroom tissue
- a plastic bottle
- a cork (fits the plastic bottle)
- a teaspoon
- a measuring cup
- vinegar
- baking soda

Steps:

1. Fold up the bathroom tissue to make a sachet to contain 1 teaspoon of baking soda.

2. Pour 80 mL of vinegar into the plastic bottle and put the packet of baking soda in it.

3. Insert the cork into the bottle quickly.

4. Observe what happens inside the bottle and watch the cork popping out of the bottle.

_____

_____

_____

Checklist

Are you able to...

- [ ] identify energy suppliers?
- [ ] define, identify, and give examples of different forms of energy?
- [ ] identify kinetic energy and potential energy?
- [ ] find the energy input and energy output for different energy converters?

Conservation of Energy (2)

I know...sun to wheat... wheat to us...

Most of the energy on Earth comes from the sun. Plants use energy from the sun to make energy-rich food for themselves to live. That energy is passed on to the organisms that eat plants. In this way, energy flows through a food chain or web.

In this unit, students will:

- learn about energy chains.
- identify different energy sources.
- distinguish between renewable and non-renewable sources of energy.
- recognize some facts about fossil fuels, coal, natural gas, and oil.

ISBN: 978-1-927042-87-8

10

A. **Draw the missing link in each energy chain. Then answer the question.**

1.

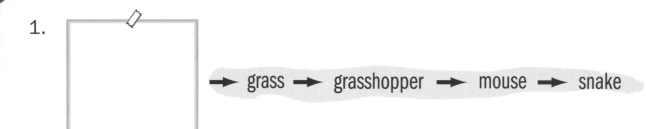

➡ grass ➡ grasshopper ➡ mouse ➡ snake

2.

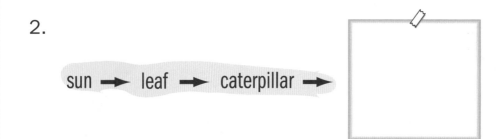

sun ➡ leaf ➡ caterpillar ➡

3.

sun ➡ plant ➡ dragonfly ➡ frog ➡

4.

In each of the above energy chains, the last "link" does not receive all the energy that comes from the sun. Why is that? (Hint: You have to eat food every day to live. Where did the energy from the food that you ate yesterday go?)

_____

_____

B. **Make an energy chain with 4 links.**

➡   ➡   ➡

_____   _____   _____   _____

ISBN: 978-1-927042-87-8

C. Match the names of the energy sources with the correct pictures.

wind   hydroelectric   natural gas

solar   coal   biomass   oil

1.

_____

2.

_____

3.

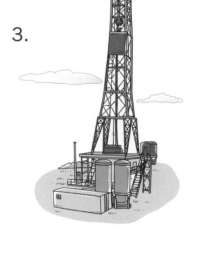

_____

4.

_____

5.

_____

6.

_____

7.

_____

10

D. Tell whether each energy source is renewable or non-renewable.

> Non-renewable energy comes from sources that cannot be made new again once the energy has been removed from them. Renewable energy is constantly being replaced.

1. oil _____

2. coal _____

3. solar _____

4. wind _____

5. biomass _____

6. hydroelectric _____

7. natural gas _____

E. Look at the headings and descriptions of some articles in _Energy Magazine_. Identify the renewable energy described. Write the answers on the lines.

municipal solid waste   geothermal   wave and tidal

1. **Waves**
   vs
   Tides

   _____ energy
   - It's wind power versus moon power in the surfing event of the year!

2. **Steamland**

   _____
   energy
   - Can the contestants use the ground source heat pumps to supply their tribes' energy? Read and find out.

3. **EFMW** Squad

   _____ energy
   - Dance to the beats of "Paper, Wood Chips, and Food" as you learn the latest from the Landfill Gas.

F. Check the ones that are true.

1. Fossil fuels:

(A) are coal, oil, and natural gas. They are burned to release heat energy. They will not last forever.

(B) are kind to the environment.

(C) were formed from the remains of prehistoric plants and animals under great pressure and heat.

2. Coal:

(A) was used at one time to heat homes and run the machines of factories but is mainly used to produce electricity.

(B) is the most plentiful and commonly used fossil fuel. It produces acid rain when burned.

(C) has a limited effect on the environment.

3. Natural gas:

(A) is pulled up from the ground and transported in pipes.

(B) contains a gas called hydrogen sulphide. It is highly toxic.

(C) will last forever.

4. Oil:

(A) is the raw material from which gasoline, jet fuel, and plastics come. It is pulled up from underground by pumps.

(B) is a very safe source of energy because it poses no threat to the Earth.

(C) is transported all over the Earth by truck, train, and ship.

10

We Use Energy

> We depend on energy for so many things.

In the following chart, list 8 things that you did in the past 12 hours. Check the ones that involved the use of energy.

Eight Things I Did in the Past 12 Hours

Activity	Energy Dependent

Are you able to...

- [ ] tell about energy chains?
- [ ] identify different energy sources?
- [ ] distinguish between renewable and non-renewable sources of energy?
- [ ] recognize some facts about fossil fuels, coal, natural gas, and oil?

ISBN: 978-1-927042-87-8

A. Complete the crossword puzzle.

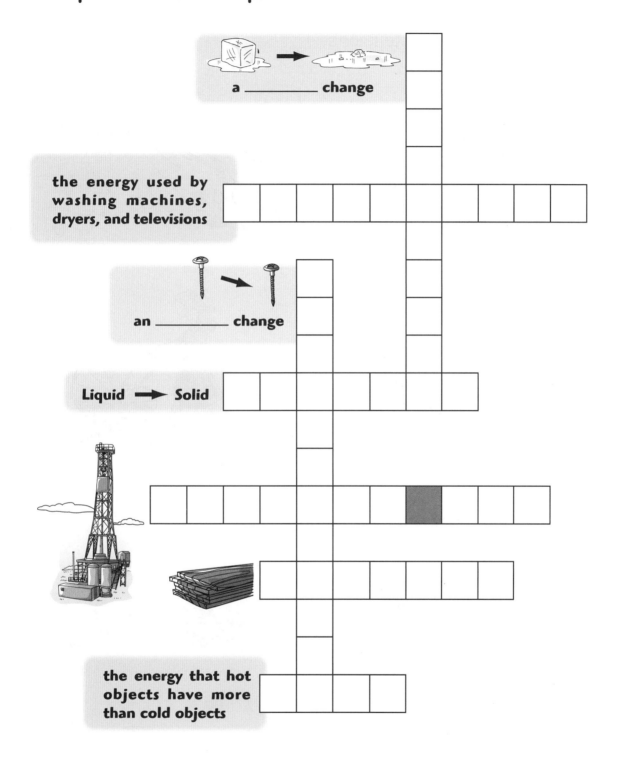

a _____ change

the energy used by washing machines, dryers, and televisions

an _____ change

Liquid ➡ Solid

the energy that hot objects have more than cold objects

biomass   freezes   electrical

heat   irreversible   natural gas   reversible

B. Check the correct answers.

1. The pictures that show tensions:

2. The ones that show reversible change:

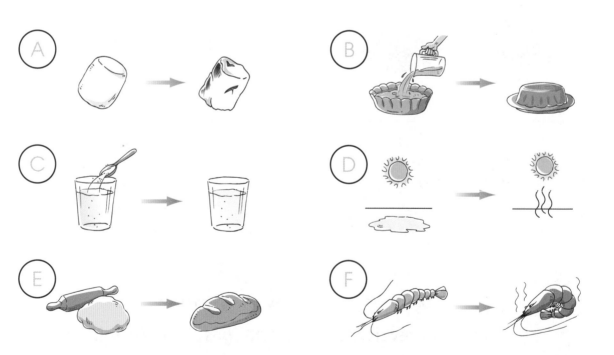

ISBN: 978-1-927042-87-8

3. The non-renewable energy sources:

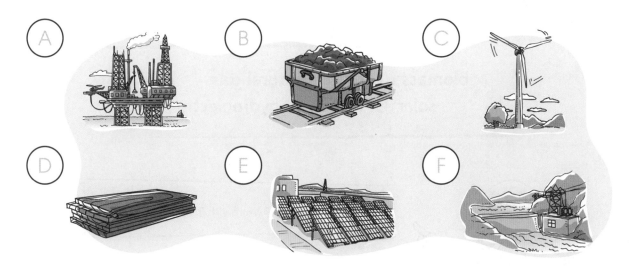

4. The sentences that describe the force of gravity:

A   It is a pushing force.

B   It is the force that pulls objects upon other objects.

C   Sir Isaac Newton was the first person to describe the force of gravity.

D   It is the force that acts on moving objects.

5. The force(s) that the picture shows:

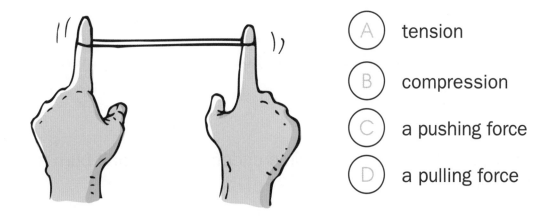

A   tension

B   compression

C   a pushing force

D   a pulling force

ISBN: 978-1-927042-87-8

C. **Guess what energy source each child represents. Write the answer on the line.**

> biomass   oil   natural gas   coal
> solar   wind   hydroelectric

1.

Gasoline, heating oil, airplane fuel...I'm in 'em all!

_____

2.

Everyone calls me "Windy".

_____

3. Darren says, "Fast water turbine... poetic, isn't it?"

_____

4. Eric says, "I'm a collector...I'm a reflector...and at times, I'm a cell!"

_____

5. Jessica says, "I spend a lot of time underground. Don't burn me up. I'll rain ACID!"

_____

ISBN: 978-1-927042-87-8

D.   Name the type of energy shown in each picture.   Use each word once.

gravitational   sound   heat   light
chemical   kinetic   electrical

1.

_____

2.

_____

3.

_____

4.

a. _____

b. _____

c. _____

d. _____

E. **Identify the part of the body that does each of the following jobs. Fill in the blanks with the given words.**

> kidney   stomach   bladder   spinal cord
>
> small intestine   skin   heart

1. _____ :

   an organ where gastric juices help break down food

2. _____ :

   an organ that pumps blood

3. _____ :

   keeps water from getting in and fluids from leaving the body

4. _____ :

   the brain communicates with the nerves through this

5. _____ :

   cleans the blood and gets rid of waste material

6. an organ where the most absorption takes place

   _____

7. a muscular organ that stores urine excreted by the kidneys

   _____

Answers

ISBN: 978-1-927042-87-8

✓ ANSWERS

1 Human Body Systems

A. 1. brain ; nervous system
2. lungs ; respiratory system
3. heart ; circulatory system
4. kidneys ; urinary system
5. bones ; skeletal system
6. stomach ; digestive system

B. 1. digestive system
2. circulatory system
3. nervous system
4. urinary system
5. skeletal system
6. respiratory system

C. 1. heartbeat   2. breathing
3. digestion   4. thought
5. emotion   6. 41
7. 100 billion   8. 1.4
9. 50 000

D. 1. oxygen   2. carbon dioxide
3. circulatory   4. diseases
5. ✔   6. ✔
7. ✗   8. ✗
9. ✔   10. ✔

Try this!
Activity

2 Respiratory System and Skeletal System

A. oxygen ; carbon dioxide
1. nose   2. lungs
3. trachea   4. bronchial tubes
5. bronchioles   6. diaphragm
7. alveoli

B. 1. nose   2. bronchial tubes
3. diaphragm   4. lungs
5. trachea   6. bronchioles
7. alveoli

C. 1. support   2. organs
3. muscles

4.

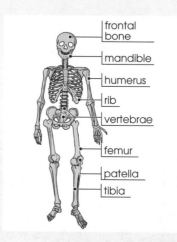

frontal
bone
mandible
humerus
rib
vertebrae
femur
patella
tibia

D. 1. Muscles   2. hollow
3. cartilage   4. 20
5. Marrow   6. thigh bone

Try this!
Activity

3 Digestive System and Excretory System

A. 1. food   2. cells
3. energy
4.

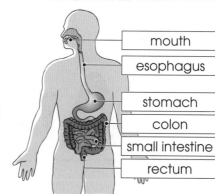

mouth
esophagus
stomach
colon
small intestine
rectum

B. 2 ; 3 ; 1 ; 6 ; 5 ; 4
C. 1. small intestine   2. colon

ISBN: 978-1-927042-87-8

D.

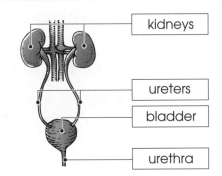

kidneys

ureters

bladder

urethra

E. 1. filter the blood and remove waste materials in the form of urine
2. stores the urine
3. allow the urine to travel down to the bladder from the kidneys
4. carries the urine away from the bladder and out of the body
F. 1. kidneys, lungs, and skin
2. lungs
3. kidneys
4. skin

Try this!
Activity

4   Nutrition

A. (Individual drawing for each source of nutrient)
1. vitamins   2. water
3. fats   4. minerals
5. carbohydrates   6. proteins
B. (Suggested answers)
1. minerals ; vitamins
2. carbohydrates ; fibre
3. fats ; minerals
C. 1. Lucy
2. (Answer will vary, but there should be more vegetables and fruits.)
D. (Individual answer)
Healthful Snack Foods: B ; C ; F

Try this!
(Individual answer)

5   Properties of Matter

A. (Suggested answer for each example)
1. liquid ; definite ; **juice**
2. gas ; no definite ; **oxygen**
3. solid ; volume ; shape ; **a pen**
B. 1. melt   2. freeze
3. evaporate   4. melt
5. freeze
C. 1. solid ; heat given ; liquid
2. solid ; heat given ; liquid
3. liquid ; heat given ; gas
4. liquid ; heat taken away ; solid
D. 1. condenses
2. evaporates
3. melts
4. freezes
5. changes ; temperatures
E.

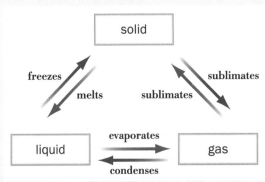

Try this!
Activity

✓ ANSWERS

Midway Review

A.

```
              D           S
              I           T
      B       A           O
      R       P           M
  C A R B O H Y D R A T E S
      I       R       C   S
      N       A       H   O
              G           P
        F E M U R         H
                          A
          C A R T I L A G E
                          U
        E V A P O R A T E S
```

B. 1. A ; C ; E ; F   2. A ; D
    3. A ; C ; D   4. A
    5. A ; B ; F   6. D
    7. C
C. Skeletal System: rib ; cartilage ; vertebra
    Circulatory System: heart ; artery ; vein
    Nervous System: spinal cord ; brain ; optic nerve
    Digestive System: esophagus ; stomach ; small
    intestine
    Urinary System: kidney ; ureter ; bladder
    Respiratory System: lung ; nose ; bronchiole

6   Changes in Matter

A. 1. chemical   2. physical
    3. colour   4. state
    5. physical change   6. chemical change
    7. chemical change   8. physical change
B. 1. reversible   2. irreversible
    3. reversible   4. reversible
    5. irreversible
C. 1. C   2. A
    3. B   4. C
    5. B   6. A
D. D, B, C, A
E. 1. 110 g   2. stayed the same
    3. 250 g   4. stayed the same

Try this!
    honey, water, oil

7   Forces and Structures (1)

A. 1. Sir Isaac Newton
    2. He saw an apple fall from a tree.
    3. The force of gravity pulled the apple to the
        ground.
    4. It is the force that pulls objects upon other
        objects.
B.

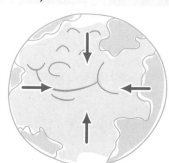

C. 1. Newton   2. inclined plane
    3. Torque   4. spoke
D. 1. force of gravity
    2-3. compression/tension
    4. pushing
    5. pulling
    6. compression
    7. tension
    8. compression
    9. tension
E. 1a. tension   b. compression
    c. compression   d. tension
    2a. compression   b. tension

Try this!
    (Individual design)

ISBN: 978-1-927042-87-8

8 Forces and Structures (2)

A. 1. B   2. C
3. These machines have greater mechanical advantage.
B. 1. ✔
2. ✘ ; Systems with more than one pulley have greater mechanical advantage.
3. ✘ ; Mechanical advantage can be gained by using gears of different sizes.
C. Trace the dotted lines.
  1. computer   2. mixer
  3. amplifier   4. speaker system
  5. CD player   6. microphone
  7. electric guitar and keyboard
  8. There are eight components.
  9. It must be able to withstand the forces from dropping or smashing.
 10. (Suggested answer)
    The power of the amplifier is turned off or the amplifier is broken.
 11. It would decrease the effectiveness of the system.

Try this!

We needed the least effort to pull up the can by using the longest board because when we increase the distance the load travels, we gain mechanical advantage.

9 Conservation of Energy (1)

A. 1. wood   2. batteries
3. food   4. gasoline
5. wind   6. the sun
B. 1. chemical   2. gravitational
3. wind   4. sound
5. heat   6. electrical
7. light
C. (Individual answers)
D. 1. kinetic   2. Potential
3. potential   4. kinetic
5. kinetic   6. potential
E. 1. electrical ; heat
2. gravitational ; electrical
3. chemical ; light and heat
4. electrical ; sound

Try this!

A gas (carbon dioxide) is produced. As the gas forms, the pressure inside the bottle builds until it pops the cork of the bottle. The forms of energy involved in this experiment are chemical energy and kinetic energy.

10 Conservation of Energy (2)

A. 1.

(Suggested drawings for questions 2 and 3)
2.   3.

4. All the plants and animals in each link need to consume the energy to live.
B. (Individual answer)
C. 1. biomass   2. coal
3. natural gas   4. solar
5. hydroelectric   6. oil
7. wind
D. 1. non-renewable 2. non-renewable
3. renewable   4. renewable
5. renewable   6. renewable
7. non-renewable
E. 1. wave and tidal   2. geothermal
3. municipal solid waste
F. 1. A ; C   2. A ; B
3. A ; B   4. A ; C

Try this!

(Individual answer)

 **ANSWERS**

Final Review

A.

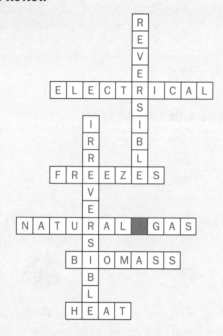

B. 1. B ; C   2. B ; C ; D
   3. A ; B   4. B ; C
   5. A ; D

C. 1. oil   2. wind
   3. hydroelectric   4. solar
   5. coal

D. 1. electrical
   2. heat
   3. light
 4a. sound
   b. kinetic
   c. chemical
   d. gravitational

E. 1. stomach   2. heart
   3. skin   4. spinal cord
   5. kidney   6. small intestine
   7. bladder

ISBN: 978-1-927042-87-8